How to be Brilliant at
CHRISTMAS TIME

Val Edgar

Brilliant Publications

We hope you and your class enjoy using this book. Other books in the series include:

Maths titles
How to be Brilliant at Using a Calculator   1 897675 04 6
How to be Brilliant at Algebra   1 897675 05 4
How to be Brilliant at Numbers   1 897675 06 2
How to be Brilliant at Shape and Space   1 897675 07 0
How to be Brilliant at Mental Arithmetic   1 897675 21 6

Science titles
How to be Brilliant at Recording in Science   1 897675 10 0
How to be Brilliant at Science Investigations 1 897675 11 9
How to be Brilliant at Materials   1 897675 12 7
How to be Brilliant at Electricity, Light and Sound   1 897675 13 5

English titles
How to be Brilliant at Writing Stories   1 897675 00 3
How to be Brilliant at Writing Poetry   1 897675 01 1
How to be Brilliant at Grammar   1 897675 02 X
How to be Brilliant at Making Books   1 897675 03 8
How to be Brilliant at Spelling   1 897675 08 9
How to be Brilliant at Reading   1 897675 09 7

If you would like further information on these or other titles published by Brilliant Publications, please write to the address given below.

Published by Brilliant Publications,
The Old School Yard, Leighton Road, Northall,
Dunstable, Bedfordshire LU6 2HA

Written by Val Edgar
Illustrated by Darin Mount
Cover photograph by Martyn Chillmaid

Printed in Malta by Interprint Ltd

© Val Edgar 1999
ISBN 1 897675 63 1

First published 1999
Reprinted 2000, 2001, 2002
10 9 8 7 6 5 4

Contents

Introduction

Christmas in the primary classroom can be a busy, stressful time, with teachers juggling the demands of the National Curriculum / 5 – 14 Guidelines with time-consuming seasonal activities.

How to be Brilliant at Christmas Time has been written by a working primary teacher, who appreciates the need for Christmas activities that are great fun, easily administered and also worthwhile and relevant within the curriculum.

The majority of these photocopiable sheets involve **Language** or **Maths** activities. The **General** section includes religious and moral education, art and design and other curriculum areas.

Every sheet stands alone as a complete activity, or can be part of a mini-Christmas theme.

Some of the sheets work particularly well with pairs or groups, especially if enlarged:

Christmas pudding (page 8)	Co-ordinates (pages 11 and 12)
Colour codes (page 14)	Christmas tree pizza toasts (page 40)
Research (page 41)	Where in the world? (page 42)
Design (page 45)	

Those sheets with a ***challenge*** offer a thought-provoking activity for the children:

Crackers (page 5)	Symmetry (page 6)
Number codes (page 10)	Dot-to-dot (page 13)
Anagrams and puzzles (page 23)	The first Christmas card (page 27)
Light (page 37)	Where in the world? (page 42)

Several of the sheets encompass religious education. A mini-topic can be followed which develops familiarity with Advent and Christmas and the customs, symbols and story associated with it, as well as an understanding of the importance of Christian moral values:

The birth of Jesus (pages 31 and 32)	Story in pictures (page 33)
Celebrating (page 35)	Advent (page 36)
Light (page 37)	Christmas fives (page 39)
Research (page 41)	Poster (page 44)

The **Worksheet follow-ups** (page 46) offers extension activities for a selection of sheets, while the **Further ideas** (page 47) suggests some extra activities for the Christmas period.

Crackers

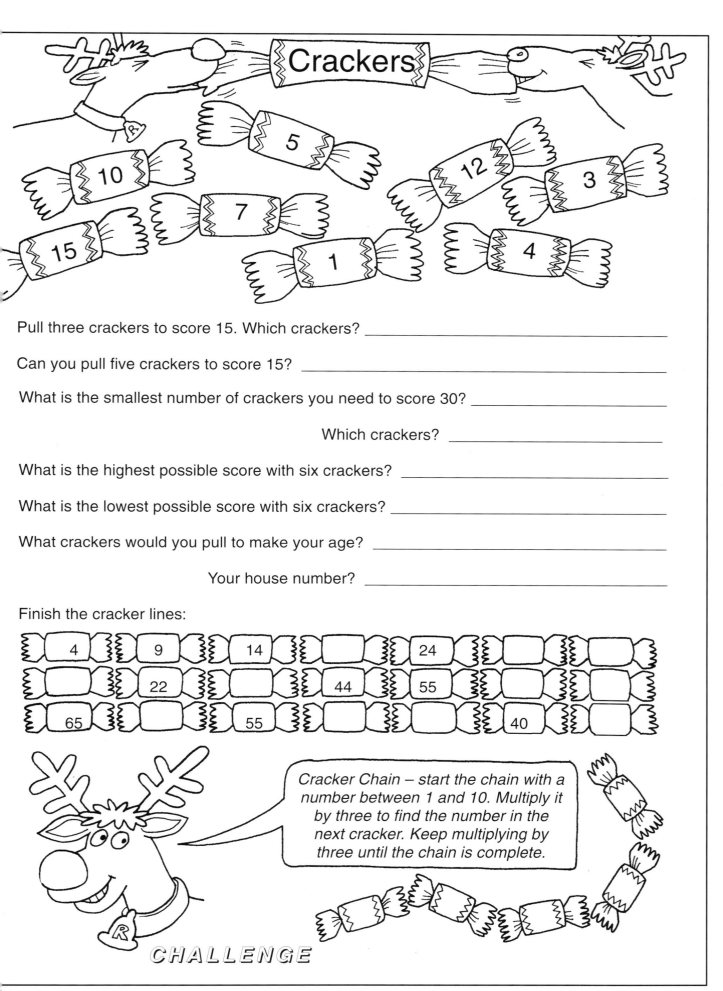

Pull three crackers to score 15. Which crackers? _____

Can you pull five crackers to score 15? _____

What is the smallest number of crackers you need to score 30? _____

Which crackers? _____

What is the highest possible score with six crackers? _____

What is the lowest possible score with six crackers? _____

What crackers would you pull to make your age? _____

Your house number? _____

Finish the cracker lines:

4	9	14		24		
22		44	55		
65		55		40	

Cracker Chain – start the chain with a number between 1 and 10. Multiply it by three to find the number in the next cracker. Keep multiplying by three until the chain is complete.

CHALLENGE

Symmetry

Follow the key at the bottom of the page to colour the picture. Draw the other half to complete the face.

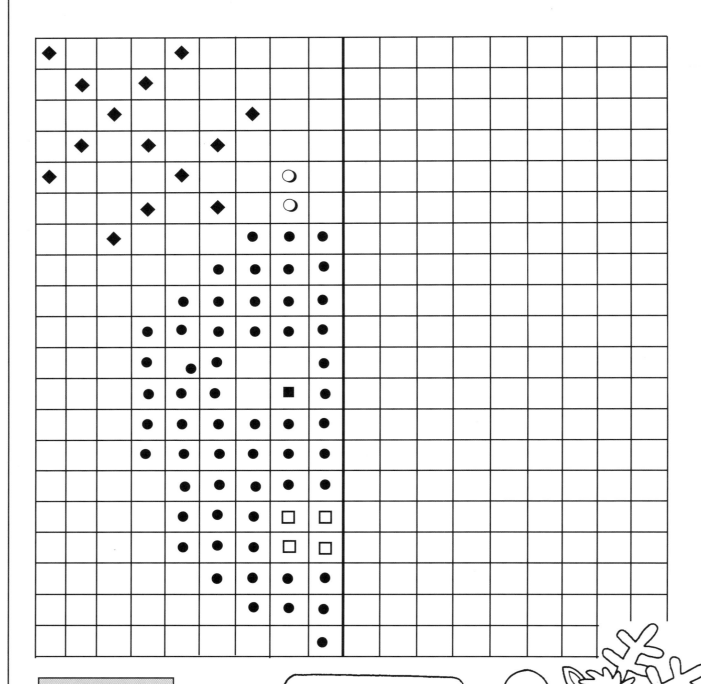

- ● **light brown**
- ◆ **dark brown**
- □ **red**
- ■ **black**
- ◖ **pink**

Use squared paper. Colour the squares to create a symmetrical Santa face.

CHALLENGE

Quick sums

Cracker 1

3	x	6	=
2	+	10	=
14	−	9	=
30	÷	3	=
2	x	8	=
1/2	of	40	=
32	−	16	=
5	+	16	=
22	−	19	=
15	+	18	=
9	x	3	=
40	−	9	=
5	x	9	=
1/2	of	30	=
17	+	22	=
38	−	16	=
40	÷	5	=
2	x	8	=
18	÷	3	=
40	+	26	=

score   =   / 20

Cracker 2

4	x	8	=
20	+	19	=
28	÷	4	=
1/2	of	24	=
19	+	27	=
40	−	11	=
5	x	6	=
32	÷	4	=
3	x	9	=
22	−	9	=
1/2	of	16	=
3	x	4	=
36	+	19	=
90	÷	10	=
8	x	3	=
100	−	27	=
36	÷	4	=
20	+	16	=
1/2	of	42	=
10	x	8	=

score   =   / 20

Christmas pudding

How many sums can you find in the Christmas pudding?

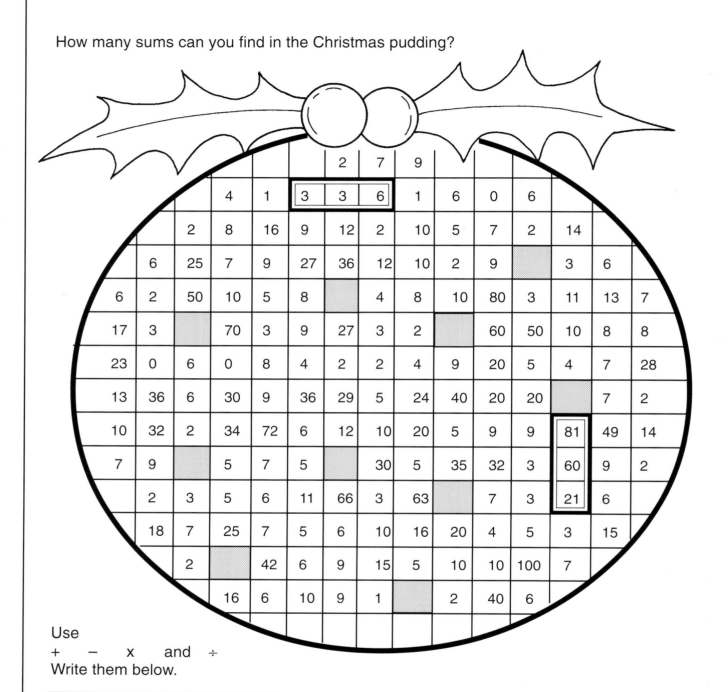

Use
+   −   x   and   ÷
Write them below.

```
3 + 3 = 6
81 − 60 = 21
```

3D Christmas tree

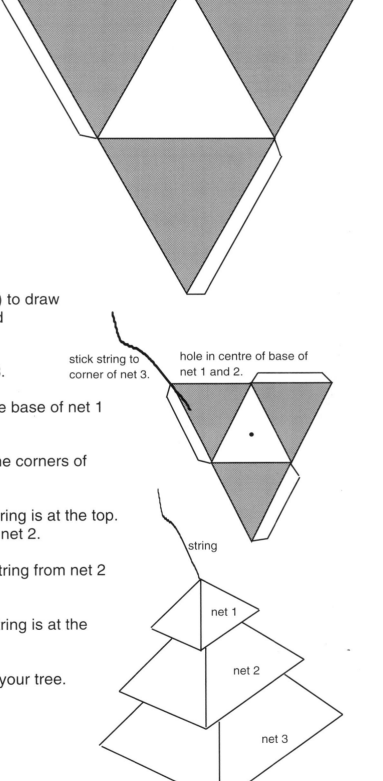

stick string to
corner of net 3.

hole in centre of base of
net 1 and 2.

string

net 1

net 2

net 3

You will need:

card (green)

3 equilateral triangles
of different sizes to draw
around

glue, scissors, string

Instructions

1. Use your smallest triangle (triangle 1) to draw
    the net of a triangular prism on a card
    (see above).

2. Draw larger nets for triangles 2 and 3.

3. Make a small hole in the middle of the base of net 1
    and net 2, as shown in the diagram.

4. Stick a length of string on to one of the corners of
    net 3.

5. Fold up and stick net 3, so that the string is at the top.
    Thread the string through the hole in net 2.

6. Fold up and stick net 2. Thread the string from net 2
    through the hole in net 1.

7. Fold up and stick net 1, so that the string is at the
    top.

8. Use the string from net 1 to hang up your tree.
    Decorate with paper decorations.

How to be Brilliant at Christmas Time

Number codes

R	P	A	N	Y	S	I	T	M	G	E	L	H	O	W
12	9	24	20	36	30	14	10	40	16	32	42	6	8	18

Crack the code to find six Christmas words.

5 x 6   6 x 4   2 x 10   5 x 2   2 x 12
S

3 x 8   5 x 4   4 x 4   4 x 8   6 x 7

3 x 3   4 x 3   4 x 8   6 x 5   8 x 4   10 x 2   10 x 1

6 x 1   4 x 2   6 x 7   7 x 6   4 x 9

10 x 4   7 x 2   3 x 10   10 x 1   6 x 7   4 x 8   2 x 5   8 x 1   4 x 8

6 x 5   5 x 4   4 x 2   9 x 2   5 x 8   4 x 6   10 x 2

Can you write the number code for these words?

STAR

TINSEL

MANGER

CHALLENGE

Co-ordinates

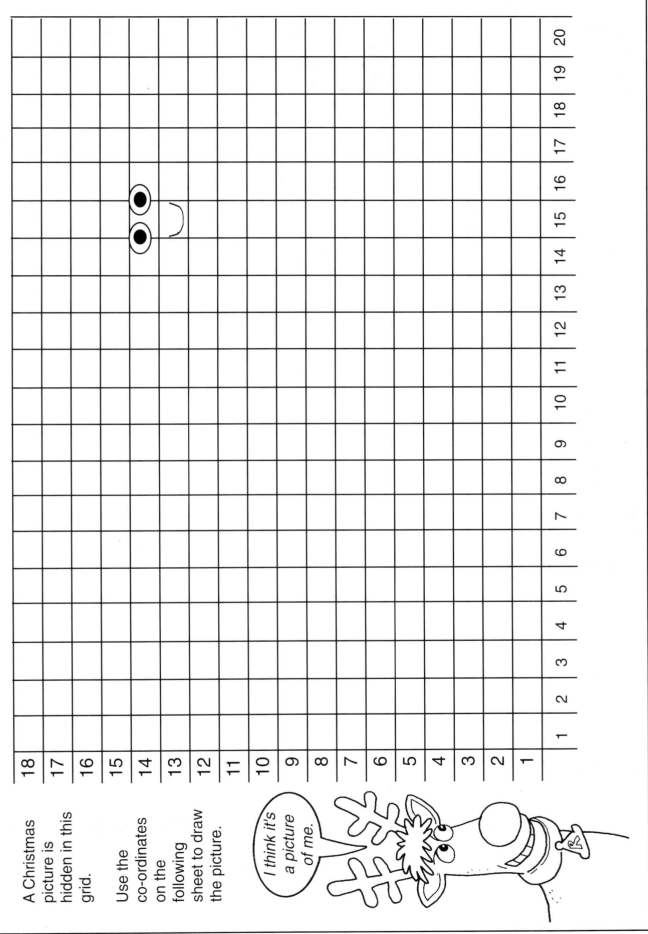

A Christmas picture is hidden in this grid.

Use the co-ordinates on the following sheet to draw the picture.

I think it's a picture of me.

Co-ordinates

Co-ordinates = (along, up)

Green:
(1,5) (2,5) (2,6) (2,9)
(3,5) (3,6) (3,7) (3,9) (3,10) (3,13)
(4,5) (4,7) (4,8) (4,9) (4,10) (4,11) (4,13) (4,14)
(5,5) (5,6) (5,8) (5,9) (5,10) (5,11) (5,12) (5,13) (5,15)
(6,5) (6,6) (6,7) (6,9) (6,10) (6,11) (6,12) (6,14) (6,15) (6,16)
(7,5) (7,6) (7,7) (7,8) (7,10) (7,11) (7,13) (7,14) (7,15)
(8,5) (8,6) (8,7) (8,8) (8,9) (8,11) (8,13) (8,14)
(9,5) (9,6) (9,7) (9,9) (9,10) (9,13)
(10,5) (10,6) (10,9) (11,5)

Yellow:
(4,6) (5,7) (5,14) (6,8) (6,13) (7,9) (7,12) (8,10)

Brown:
(5,4) (6,4) (7,4)

Red:
(3,3) (4,2) (4,3) (5,2) (5,3) (6,2) (6,3) (7,2) (7,3) (8,2) (8,3) (9,3)
(13,7) (13,8) (13,9) (13,10) (13,11)
(14,4) (14,5) (14,6) (14,8) (14,9) (14,10) (14,11)
(15,4) (15,5) (15,6) (15,8) (15,9) (15,10) (15,16)
(16,6) (16,8) (16,9) (16,10) (16,16) (16,17)
(17,4) (17,5) (17,6) (17,8) (17,9) (17,10) (17,15) (17,16) (17,17)
(18,4) (18,5) (18,6) (18,8) (18,9) (18,10) (18,11) (18,15) (18,16) (18,17)
(19,7) (19,8) (19,9) (19,10) (19,11) (19,14) (19,15) (19,16)
(20,14) (20,15)

Pink:
(13,6) (15,13) (15,14) (16,13) (16,14) (17,13) (17,14) (19,6)

Black:
(14,2) (14,7) (15,2) (15,3) (15,7) (17,2) (17,3) (17,7) (18,2) (18,7)

White:
(14,13) (14,14) (14,15)
(15,11) (15,12) (15,15)
(16,11) (16,12) (16,15)
(17,11) (17,12)
(18,13) (18,14)
(20,13)

Colour all the remaining squares **pale blue**.
Remember – leave all **white** squares alone!

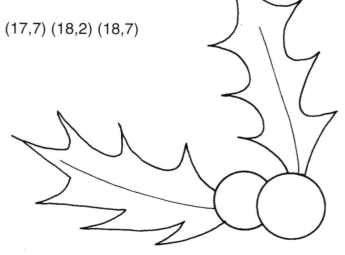

Dot-to-dot

Start at number 4 and add 3 each time.

Solve the dot-to-dot by spelling out a famous Christmas song.

CHALLENGE

How to be Brilliant at Christmas Time

Colour codes

24	red
10	yellow
40	blue
63	green
48	purple
30	orange
28	brown
54	black

7 + 3

2 x 20

1/2 of 80

4 x 10

7 x 9

1/2 of 96

50 − 22

3 x 10

6 x 4

5 x 6

1/2 of 56

4 + 4 + 2

5 + 6 + 19

4 + 6

6 x 9

14 + 14

5 x 6

24 + 16

20 + 8

13 + 15

40 − 12

17 + 11

20 + 32 + 11

6 x 8

50 − 2

10 x 4

50 − 10

6 + 6 + 6 + 6

16 + 16 + 16

100 − 37

1/2 of 60

2 x 14

Rudolph's letter

What would Rudolph like for Christmas?
Write his letter to Santa.

Think!

> Where does he live?
> What does he like to do?
> What present would he find useful?
> What present would be great fun for a reindeer?

Dear Santa,

_____

_____

_____

_____

_____

_____

love from _____

Nouns, adjectives and verbs

Look at the picture.

A **noun** is a naming word.
Write four nouns.

_____ _____

_____ _____

An **adjective** is a describing word.
Write four adjectives.

_____ _____

_____ _____

A **verb** is an action word.
Write four verbs.

_____ _____

_____ _____

Read this Christmas story.

Santa flies across the snowy rooftops in his sleigh while

the children are sleeping. He delivers presents to all the

houses before the sun rises on Christmas Day. Although it

is a cold, snowy night, the tired reindeer keep working.

They never complain. In the morning all the excited

children will jump out of bed and find gifts under the

Christmas tree or in their colourful stockings.

Underline these words:
nouns   –   red
adjectives –   blue
verbs   –   green

Dictionary skills

Use a dictionary.
Match the Christmas words with their definitions.

Advent

Yule

mistletoe

manger

Nativity

stable

the birth of Christ

a feeding box for cattle and horses

a plant with white berries which grows on other trees

a building where horses are kept

the four weeks before Christmas

the Christmas season

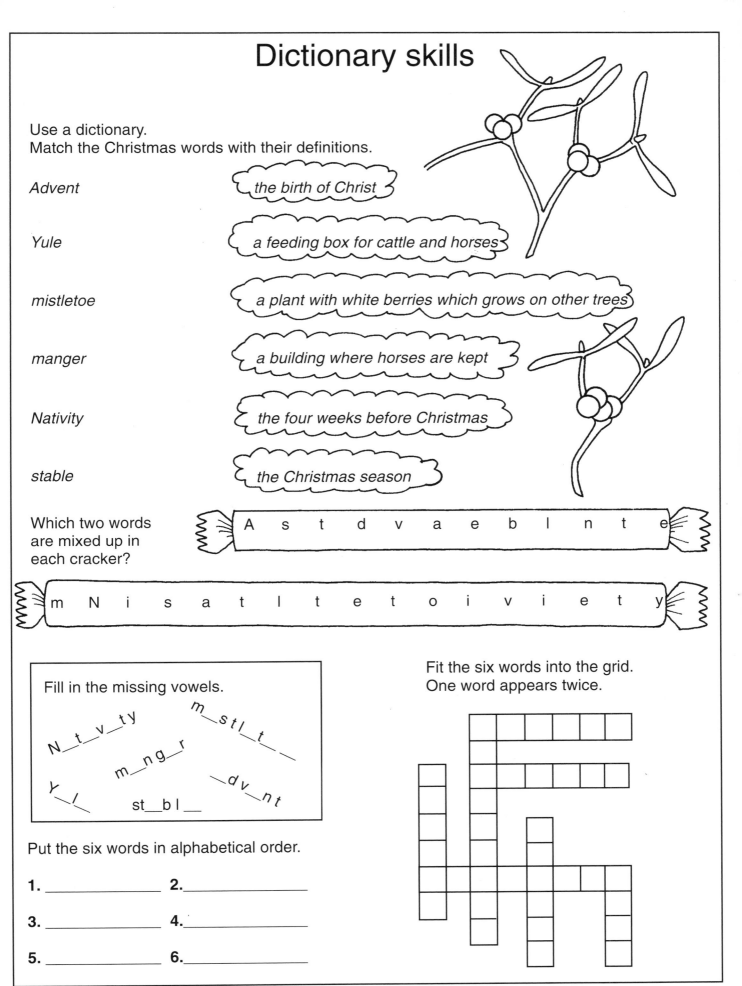

Which two words are mixed up in each cracker?

A s t d v a e b l n t e

m N i s a t l t e t o i v i e t y

Fill in the missing vowels.

N_t_v_ty   m_stl_t_

m_ng_r

Y_l_   st__bl__   _dv_nt

Put the six words in alphabetical order.

1. _____   2. _____

3. _____   4. _____

5. _____   6. _____

Fit the six words into the grid.
One word appears twice.

How to be Brilliant at Christmas Time

Cartoon strip

Stephen is building a snowman, but what is he planning to do next? Complete the cartoon strip to tell the story.

Picture poems

Christmas tree
Fill the lines with words or phrases to describe the tree.

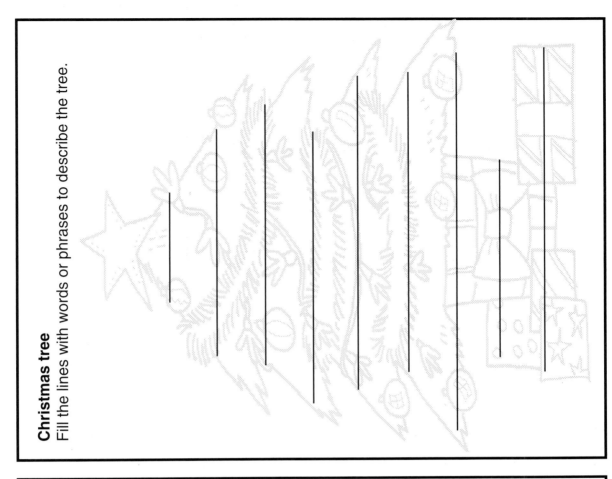

Tinsel
Continue the poem to form a long strand of tinsel.

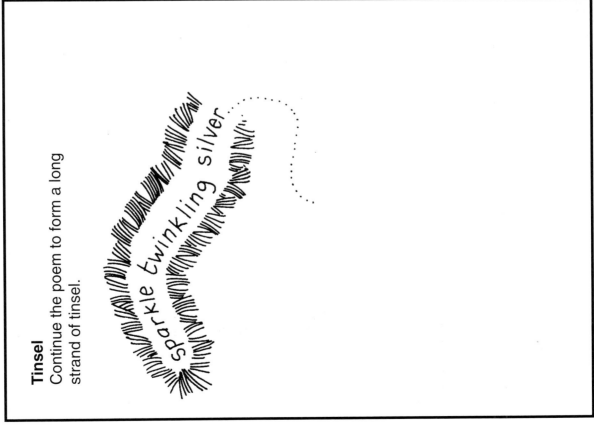

sparkle twinkling silver

Nativity search

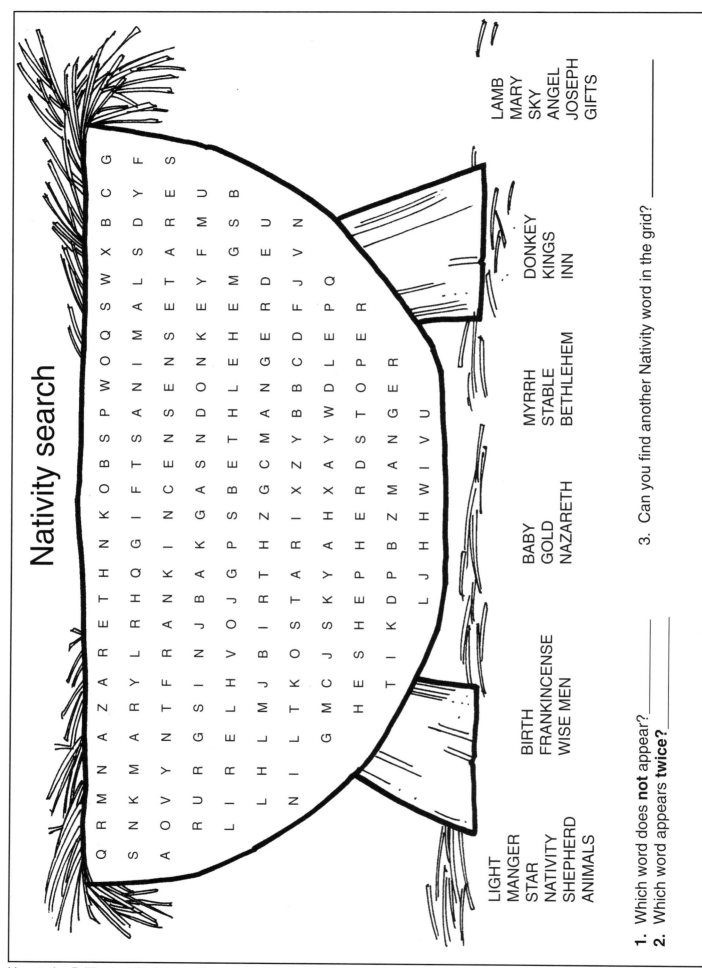

LIGHT
MANGER
STAR
NATIVITY
SHEPHERD
ANIMALS

BIRTH
FRANKINCENSE
WISE MEN

BABY
GOLD
NAZARETH

MYRRH
STABLE
BETHLEHEM

DONKEY
KINGS
INN

LAMB
MARY
SKY
ANGEL
JOSEPH
GIFTS

1. Which word does **not** appear? _____
2. Which word appears **twice**? _____
3. Can you find another Nativity word in the grid? _____

Santa's mystery letter

Oh no! Rudolph has chewed up this letter before Santa could read it. Try to fill in the missing words to help Santa.

322 Elm Aven

Santa

I have tried to be
during the last year. I help my
and play with my little bro
   For Christmas I would
to get lots of

My favourite sport is swimming
love to have a new pair of
my eyes. I would also like a

could I also ask for a rocking
for my brother. He is still too
to write to you himself.

Thank you Santa

love from
An

How to be Brilliant at Christmas Time

Rudolph's story

I have written a story to describe Christmas Eve with Santa, but I don't know how to punctuate it. Help me out, please. Santa says I have made six silly spelling mistakes. Can you find them and correct them, please?

every chistmas eve is the same santa wakes up about 12 oclock and starts bossing me about he says rudolph wake up the raindeer we have a late breakfast and start to get ready for a bisy night by about 4 oclock everything is packed on to santas sleigh and santa has finished the present list for this year our first stop is to deliver a toy cassle and scooter to 25 oak avenue barntown at about 6am santa will say arent you finished yet im tired shortly after we will fly back to the north poll and sleep for a day too recover

_____

_____

_____

_____

_____

_____

_____

_____

_____

Anagrams and puzzles

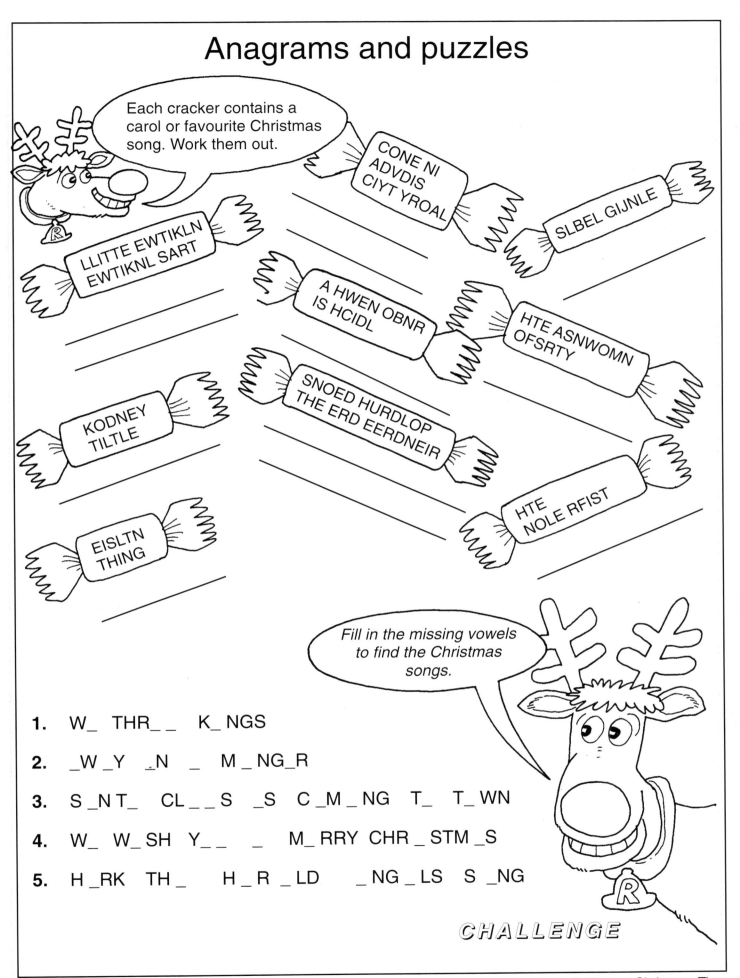

Each cracker contains a carol or favourite Christmas song. Work them out.

CONE NI
ADVDIS
CIYT YROAL

SLBEL GIJNLE

LLITTE EWTIKLN
EWTIKNL SART

A HWEN OBNR
IS HCIDL

HTE ASNWOMN
OFSRTY

KODNEY
TILTLE

SNOED HURDLOP
THE ERD EERDNEIR

HTE
NOLE RFIST

EISLTN
THING

Fill in the missing vowels to find the Christmas songs.

1. W_ THR_ _ K_NGS

2. _W _Y _N _ M_NG_R

3. S_NT_ CL_ _S _S C_M_NG T_ T_WN

4. W_ W_SH Y_ _ _ M_RRY CHR_STM_S

5. H_RK TH_ H_R_LD _NG_LS S_NG

CHALLENGE

How to be Brilliant at Christmas Time

Sabotage

Santa's sleigh has been sabotaged!

What has been done to it? Who did it? – Do we know?
Why was it done? What was the outcome? What happened to all the presents?
Did it affect the children? If so, how did they react?

Write a newspaper report about the incident.
Remember to write the headline and draw a photograph.

Christmas fun wordsheet

Christmas tree
decorations
baubles
presents
star
angel
fairy lights
tinsel

Santa Claus
beard
boots
sack
Rudolph
antlers
sleigh
reindeer

turkey
Christmas pudding
mince pie
Yule log
cracker

snowman
sledge
snowballs
snowflakes
carol singers
lantern

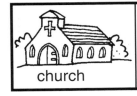

church

Advent candle

Advent calendar

Christmas card

candle

wreath

stocking

robin

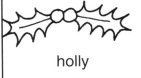

holly

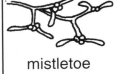

mistletoe

How to be Brilliant at Christmas Time

Adjectives

Write describing words for
each Christmas picture.

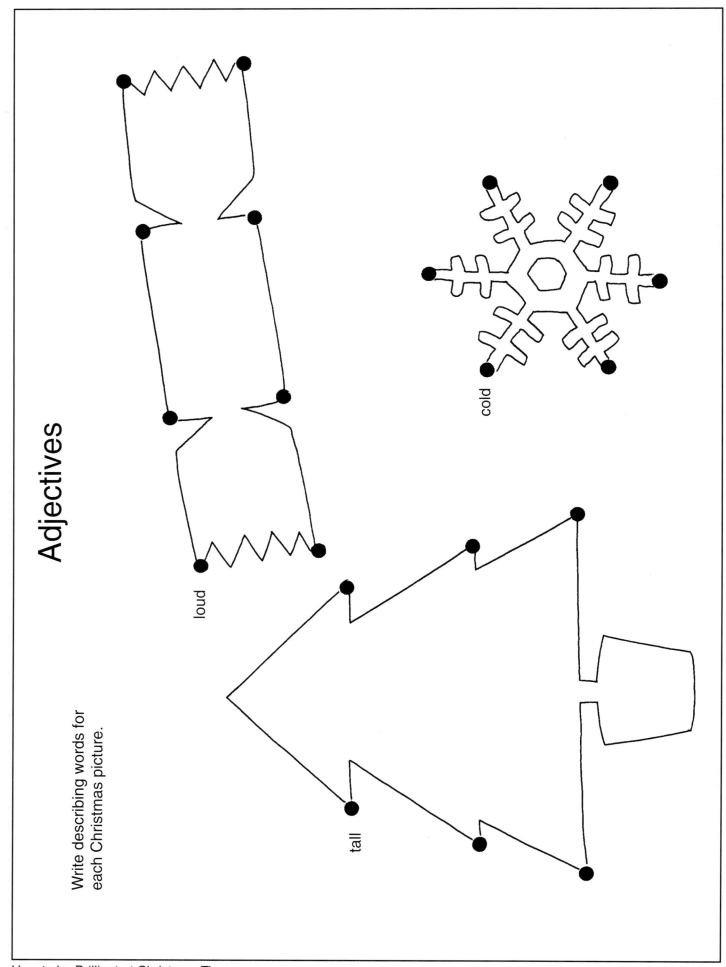

cold

loud

tall

The first Christmas card

Cut around the dotted lines and re-arrange the sentences to discover the story of the first Christmas card.

An artist drew the design for the card.

Long ago people wrote letters to each other to send their Christmas greetings.

In December 1843 a man called Henry Cole realized he did not have time to write to each of his friends.

But it was a few years before Christmas cards became really popular in Britain.

One thousand cards were printed and sold.

So he decided to make a card which could be printed many times and then sent to all his friends.

Find a picture of the first Christmas card in your Christmas books or encyclopedia.

CHALLENGE

How to be Brilliant at Christmas Time

Nativity words

Word grid

Which word is revealed?_____

Word cross

Fit the Nativity words into the word cross.

Which word fits twice? _____

Word twist

Start with **S**. Move from letter to letter finding all the words in the grid.

I	K	T	S	L	B	M
N	R	A	Y	E	A	A
G	B	A	B	G	N	L
S	D	H	P	S	E	Y
M	R	E	E	H	K	N
A	N	G	E	R	D	O

Which word is left in the word twist?

_____

Story starter

Start in the middle.

Christmas Eve

Follow the arrows to find ideas for your own story.

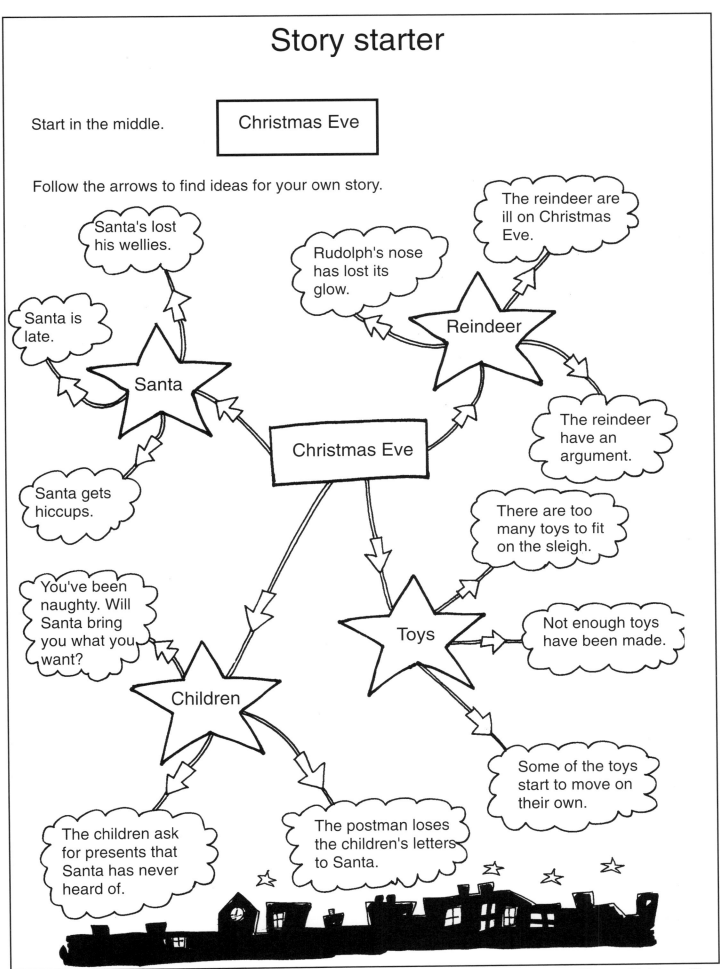

Santa's lost his wellies.

Santa is late.

Rudolph's nose has lost its glow.

The reindeer are ill on Christmas Eve.

Santa

Reindeer

Santa gets hiccups.

The reindeer have an argument.

Christmas Eve

There are too many toys to fit on the sleigh.

You've been naughty. Will Santa bring you what you want?

Toys

Not enough toys have been made.

Children

Some of the toys start to move on their own.

The children ask for presents that Santa has never heard of.

The postman loses the children's letters to Santa.

How to be Brilliant at Christmas Time

Words, words, words

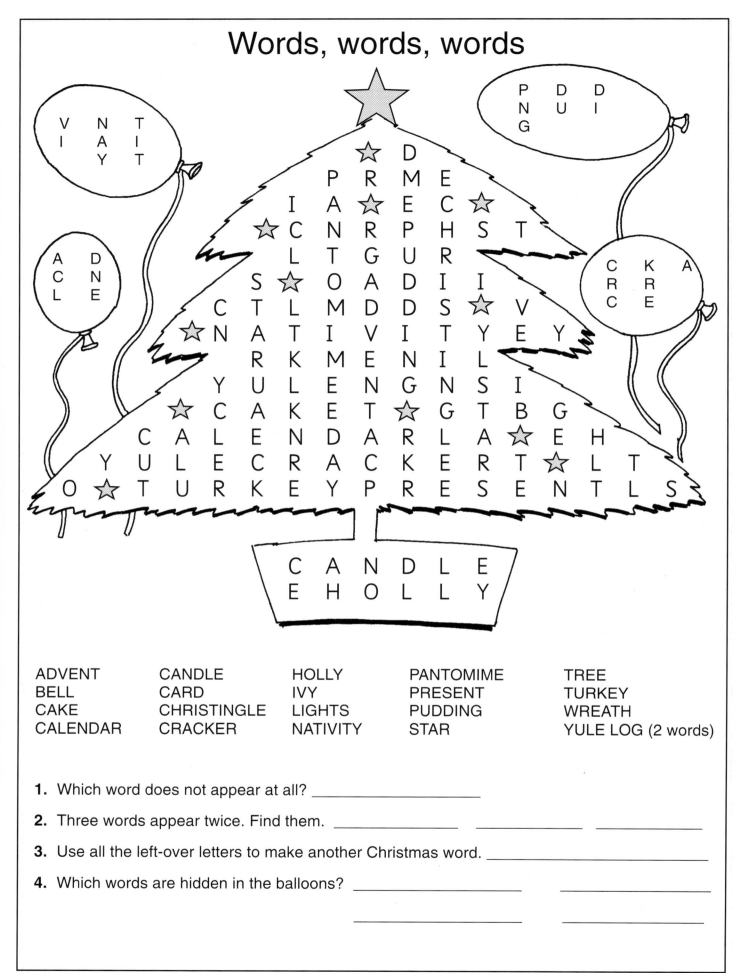

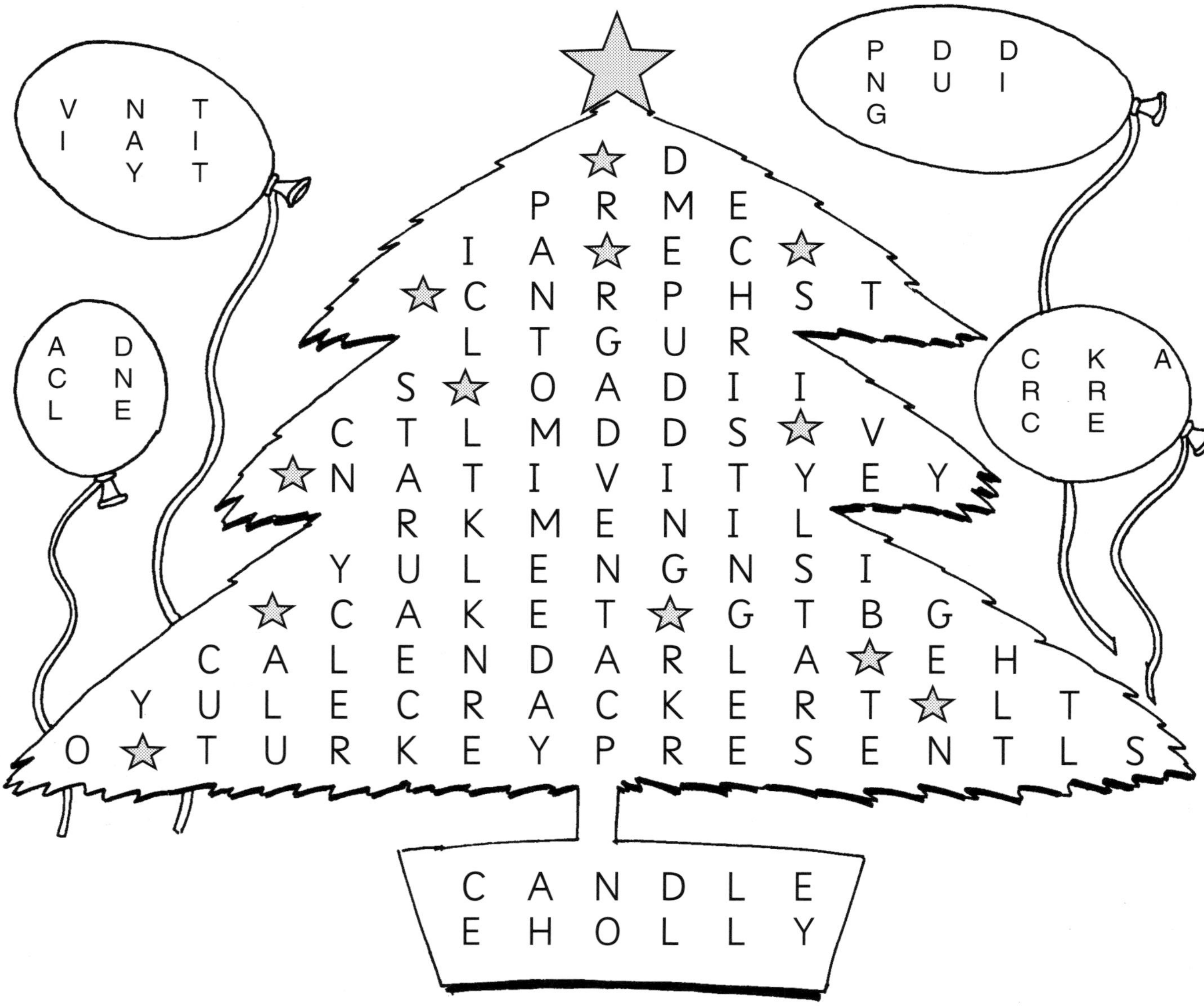
V N T
I A I
Y T
A D
C N
L E
P D D
N U I
G
C K A
R R
C E
D
P R M E
I A E C
C N R P H S T
L T G U R
S O A D I I
C T L M D D S V
N A T I V I T Y E Y
R K M E N I L
Y U L E N G N S I
C A K E T G T B G
C A L E N D A R L A E H
Y U L E C R A C K E R T L T
O T U R K E Y P R E S E N T L S
C A N D L E
E H O L L Y

ADVENT	CANDLE	HOLLY	PANTOMIME	TREE
BELL	CARD	IVY	PRESENT	TURKEY
CAKE	CHRISTINGLE	LIGHTS	PUDDING	WREATH
CALENDAR	CRACKER	NATIVITY	STAR	YULE LOG (2 words)

1. Which word does not appear at all? ____________________

2. Three words appear twice. Find them. ______________ ______________ ______________

3. Use all the left-over letters to make another Christmas word. ____________________

4. Which words are hidden in the balloons? ____________________ ____________________

____________________ ____________________

The birth of Jesus

Fill in all the missing words.

In a town called _____ there lived a girl called Mary. She was engaged to marry _____, a carpenter.

_____ day she was visited by an angel. He was the angel Gabriel, God's _____. He spoke to her, saying, 'I have a message for you from God. You _____ have a baby and he will be God's son.'

Joseph   One   will
Nazareth   messenger

_____ afterwards the Roman _____ Augustus issued an order that everyone must go to their home town to register for paying _____. So Joseph and _____ had to travel to Bethlehem.

Mary   taxes
Emperor   Soon

It was a long _____ on rough roads. _____ donkey carried the food and _____. Mary found the journey really _____ as her baby was due to be _____ very soon.

Their   journey   born
clothing   tiring

Mary arrived _____, but the inn was _____ with other travellers. The innkeeper wanted to _____ but the only space he had was ____ the stable. That night Mary's baby was _____ in the stable. She wrapped him warmly and laid him in the manger to _____.

in	**exhausted**	**born**
	full **help**	**sleep**

_____ in the hills nearby were quietly watching their sheep, when suddenly the sky lit ____. An angel spoke to them, _____ , 'God's King is born today in Bethlehem. He is _____ in a manger'. They hurried to _____ town and saw baby Jesus. When they left they _____ everyone about the angel's message and the little baby.

saying   **up**   **asleep**
Shepherds   **the**   **told**

Three _____ men from the east followed a brilliant _____ in the sky. They came to visit Jesus in the stable. They brought him _____ of gold, frankincense and myrrh. Mary never forgot these special _____ who came to see her _____.

presents   **baby**   **star**
wise   **visitors**

Story in pictures

Tell the story about the birth of Jesus in pictures. Draw what is happening in each part of the story. Use reference books, a Bible, story books or carol books for ideas about the clothing, houses, weather and countryside you would expect to see.
Cut out and re-arrange the pictures to tell the story.

The shepherds saw a bright light in the sky. An angel told them the good news.	Three wise men followed a star to the stable. They brought gifts for the baby.
There was no room at the inn, so they slept in the stable.	Mary's baby was born and laid in a manger to sleep.
Mary and Joseph travelled to Bethlehem with their donkey.	The shepherds visited the baby.

How to be Brilliant at Christmas Time

My ideal Christmas Day

Write and draw
all your ideas for
a great day.

morning

afternoon

evening

How to be Brilliant at Christmas Time

Celebrating

Which special days do you celebrate each year?

1. _____   5. _____

2. _____   6. _____

3. _____   7. _____

4. _____   8. _____

Fill the snowflake with ideas about how you celebrate Christmas.

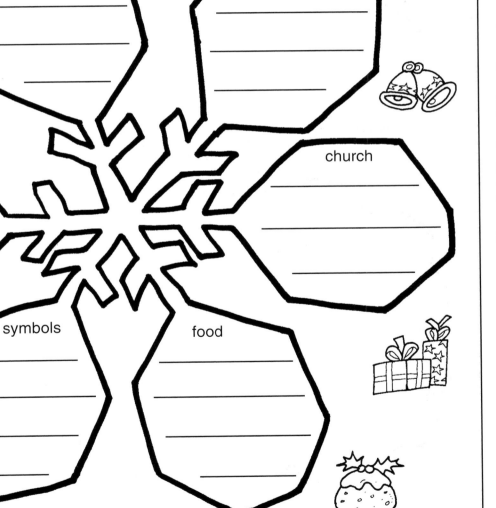

music

giving and sharing

decorations

church

symbols

food

Put a star * beside all your favourite activities.

How to be Brilliant at Christmas Time

Advent

Advent is a time of preparation.

Use the calendar below to plan what you will do during Advent: writing Christmas cards, making or buying gifts, going to parties, watching a pantomime, baking, decorating the tree, etc. (Use a blue pencil.)

Once you have planned ahead as much as you can, fill in the calendar below each day like a diary, recording all the fun you had during Advent. (Use a red pencil.)

1	2	3	4
5	6	7	8
9	10	11	12
13	14	15	16
17	18	19	20
21	22	23	24

How to be Brilliant at Christmas Time

Light

Many years ago people called pagans held great celebrations in December. It was mid-winter, and the very time when they wanted to encourage light and life to come back into their world. They lit candles, burnt logs and waited for the longer days to come.

When Christians began to celebrate the birth of Jesus, they kept many of the pagan customs and traditions in their celebrations, in particular the use of light. To Christians, light is an important aspect because it symbolizes the love of Jesus.

As celebrations have developed over the years, many homes now have Advent candles and Advent rings for a countdown to the big day; trees have fairy lights and bright stars; children make christingles and carol singers carry lanterns; windows are decorated with candles and welcome lights, and some people still burn a Yule log. Christmas without light is hard to imagine.

1.   Why do people nowadays use light to celebrate Christmas? _____

_____

2.   Use a highlight pen. Highlight all the ways YOU use light at Christmas in your home.

3.   List the ways people use light to celebrate under these two headings:

Electric light   Other fuels

_____   _____

_____   _____

_____   _____

_____   _____

_____   _____

Find out how to make a christingle.

CHALLENGE

Invitation

You are going to have a Christmas party. Design an invitation to send to your friends.

Think about all the information you will need to give. Make it really attractive.

Christmas fives

Complete these lists to show how kind and considerate you can be at Christmas.

Five things I could do to help at home.

1. _____
2. _____
3. _____
4. _____
5. _____

Five things I could do for my friends.

1. _____
2. _____
3. _____
4. _____
5. _____

Five things I could do for the elderly.

1. _____
2. _____
3. _____
4. _____
5. _____

Five things I could do to help my teacher.

1. _____
2. _____
3. _____
4. _____
5. _____

How to be Brilliant at Christmas Time

Christmas tree pizza toasts

Ingredients:
4 slices bread
tomato puree
cheese slices
tinned sweetcorn
sliced onions
chopped green pepper
sliced cherry tomatoes
dried mixed herbs

You will need:
a knife (not too sharp)
a grill (to be used with adult help)

What to do:

1. Use a knife or Christmas tree pastry cutter to cut four tree shapes from the bread.

2. Toast the bread on both sides under the grill (get an adult to help you).

3. Spread the toast with tomato puree and sprinkle lightly with herbs.

4. Add the cheese slice.

5. Decorate the trees using the remaining ingredients.

6. Toast the trees under a medium grill for a few minutes (with adult help) until the cheese bubbles.

How to be Brilliant at Christmas Time

Research

We have many ways of celebrating Christmas, but have you ever thought about why we celebrate in the way we do?

Use your Christmas reference books or encyclopedia to find out.

Find out all you can about two of these Christmas customs and celebrations.

Christmas card

Christmas tree

pantomime

Santa Claus

mistletoe

cracker

Christmas pudding

Nativity scene

Yule log

How to be Brilliant at Christmas Time

Where in the world?

Santa has been really busy this Christmas Eve.

Using a globe, find the name of every country he visited.

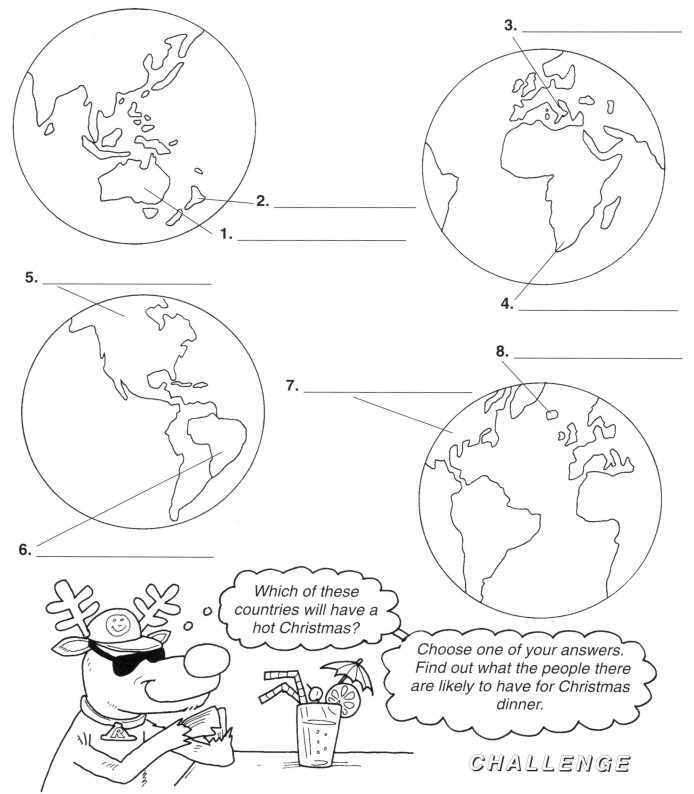

3. _____

2. _____

1. _____

4. _____

5. _____

8. _____

7. _____

6. _____

Which of these countries will have a hot Christmas?

Choose one of your answers. Find out what the people there are likely to have for Christmas dinner.

CHALLENGE

How to be Brilliant at Christmas Time

Hanging cards

Follow the flow chart to make your fold-up, fold-out card.

> Take a piece of card about 10cm wide and as long as possible.

⇩

> Fold the card first one way and then the other way, like a fan, in sections of about 15 – 20cm long.

⇩

> Press hard on all the folds to make the card lie as flat as possible.

⇩

> Draw your design on the top piece of card. Make sure a large part of the picture lies along the top and bottom edges of the card.

⇩

> Cut out the picture. Make sure you leave it joined at the edge to the card underneath.

⇩

> Draw around the picture on to the second layer of card and cut it out.

⇩

> Repeat this with every layer of card.

⇩

> Colour and add detail to the pictures on each layer and fold the card up again.

⇩

> Make a hole in the top layer and thread ribbon through to hang the card.

How to be Brilliant at Christmas Time

Poster

Everywhere I look there are posters advertising toys, food, clothes and all the other things people buy at Christmas. I wish someone would design a poster encouraging people to consider the **real** meaning of Christmas.

Design

The reindeer have a problem.

Help!
Our sleigh is too small for all the presents. Everything gets wet in the snow. A lot of houses don't have chimneys so we need to park in the gardens and travel along the roads and footpaths. The sleigh is just not suitable any more.

Design a new, spacious all-terrain vehicle for Santa and the reindeer.

Describe and draw.

_____

_____

_____

_____

_____

_____

Swap ideas with a friend and write about their sheet.

Things I liked best _____

_____

Things I would change _____

_____

Worksheet follow-ups

Symmetry – page 6
Make a display of symmetrical and asymmetrical Christmas pictures, either from Christmas cards or drawings on squared paper.

Christmas pudding – page 8
Try to find longer sums in the pudding, with four or five figures, eg $6 \times (2 \times 3) + 0 = 36$

3D Christmas tree – page 9
Repeat the activity using square pyramid nets.

Rudolph's letter – page 15
Write and send fun letters to Santa by e-mail using one of Santa's websites that are available.

Nouns, adjectives and verbs – page 16
The same activity can be very successful using Christmas card scenes.

Sabotage – page 24
Continue this theme to write articles, adverts, human interest stories, etc for a *Lapland Times* newspaper.

Christmas fun wordsheet – page 25
Use as necessary for spelling support for all writing work.

Celebrating – page 35
Review and discuss the children's answers. How many of the special days are Christian festivals? What is celebrated on the other special days? What special days do children of other religions celebrate? How?

Advent – page 36
Enlarge this sheet to make a class calendar / diary for events in your school.

Light – page 37
Make a class collection of *Light at Christmas today* and *Light at Christmas 100 years ago.*

Where in the world? – page 42
Prepare an Australian Christmas lunch.

Further ideas

Pass the mime

Play pass the parcel, except that whenever the music stops a child unwraps one sheet of paper from the parcel and finds a Christmas activity written underneath. They then must act it out for the other children to guess, for example writing cards, decorating the tree, stirring the pudding. To develop this, the children form groups of four or five, have a discussion and then each act out a Christmas activity interacting with each other to form a scene in a home, shop, school, etc. The others guess the situation and the individual mimes.

Puppet

Make a Rudolph glove puppet using a brown sock, pipe cleaners to thread through for antlers and scraps of felt for eyes and a nose. Use the puppet to tell stories.

Maps

Photocopy a map of the area where the children live. Take one familiar section, perhaps six or ten streets. Challenge the groups to work out the best route for Santa to visit all the houses in a set area in the shortest time by using the map. Compare group results and reasons for their decisions.

Game

Children can design their own Advent board game, *Countdown to Christmas.* It should include 25 squares, two dice and problems, for example Santa's lost his wellies – miss a turn. It can be as funny or as outrageous as they like.

Carol singer frieze

Each child makes a small carol singer using thick card about 40cm high. Clothe the figure using scraps of fabric, padded with newspaper where possible. Remember hats, scarves, gloves and lanterns. Mount the figures on deep blue frieze paper with silhouettes of houses and a starry sky.

Money

Give Santa £100 and a challenge. Using a catalogue he has to buy presents for an extended family within his budget. Work out his shopping list, costs and change. For an extra challenge include special offers, for example 10% off.

How to be Brilliant at Christmas Time

Answers

Crackers page 5

7, 5, 3or 10, 4, 1

no

3

15, 10, 5 or 15, 12, 3

53

30

4, 9, 14, 19, 24, 29, 34

11, 22, 33, 44, 55, 66, 77

65, 60, 55, 50, 45, 40, 35

Quick sums page 7

Cracker 1:

18, 12, 5, 10, 16, 20, 16, 21, 3, 33, 27, 31, 45, 15, 39, 22, 8, 16, 6, 66

Cracker 2:

32, 39, 7, 12, 46, 29, 30, 8, 27, 13, 8, 12, 55, 9, 24, 73, 9, 36, 21, 80

Number codes page 10

Santa, angel, present, holly, mistletoe, snowman

Dot-to-dot page 13

snowflake   Rudolph the red nosed reindeer (cracker)

Dictionary skills pg 17

Advent – the four weeks...   Yule – the Christmas...

mistletoe – a plant with...   manger – a feeding box...

Nativity – the birth of...   stable – a building…

Advent / stable   mistletoe / Nativity

1. Advent
2. manger
3. mistletoe
4. Nativity
5. stable
6. Yule

Nativity Search page 20

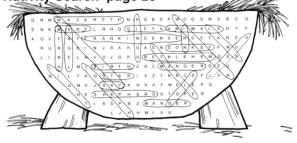

1. baby   2. manger   3. Jesus

Words, words, words page 30

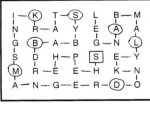

1. wreath
2. cake, star, Yule
3. mistletoe
4. Nativity, pudding, candle, cracker

Anagrams and puzzles page 23

Twinkle, twinkle little star

Little donkey

Silent night

Once in royal David's city

When a child is born

Rudolph the red nosed reindeer

Jingle bells

Frosty the snowman

The first noel

1. We three kings
2. Away in a manger
3. Santa Claus is coming to town
4. We wish you a merry Christmas
5. Hark the herald angels sing

The first Christmas card page 27

Long ago...

In December...

So he...

An artist...

One thousand...

But it...

Where in the world? page 42

1. Australia   2. New Zealand
3. Italy   4. South Africa
5. Canada   6. Brazil
7. U.S.A.   8. Iceland

Australia, New Zealand, South Africa, Brazil

Nativity words page 28

Word grid – manger

Word cross – baby

Word twist – angel

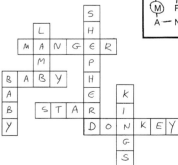